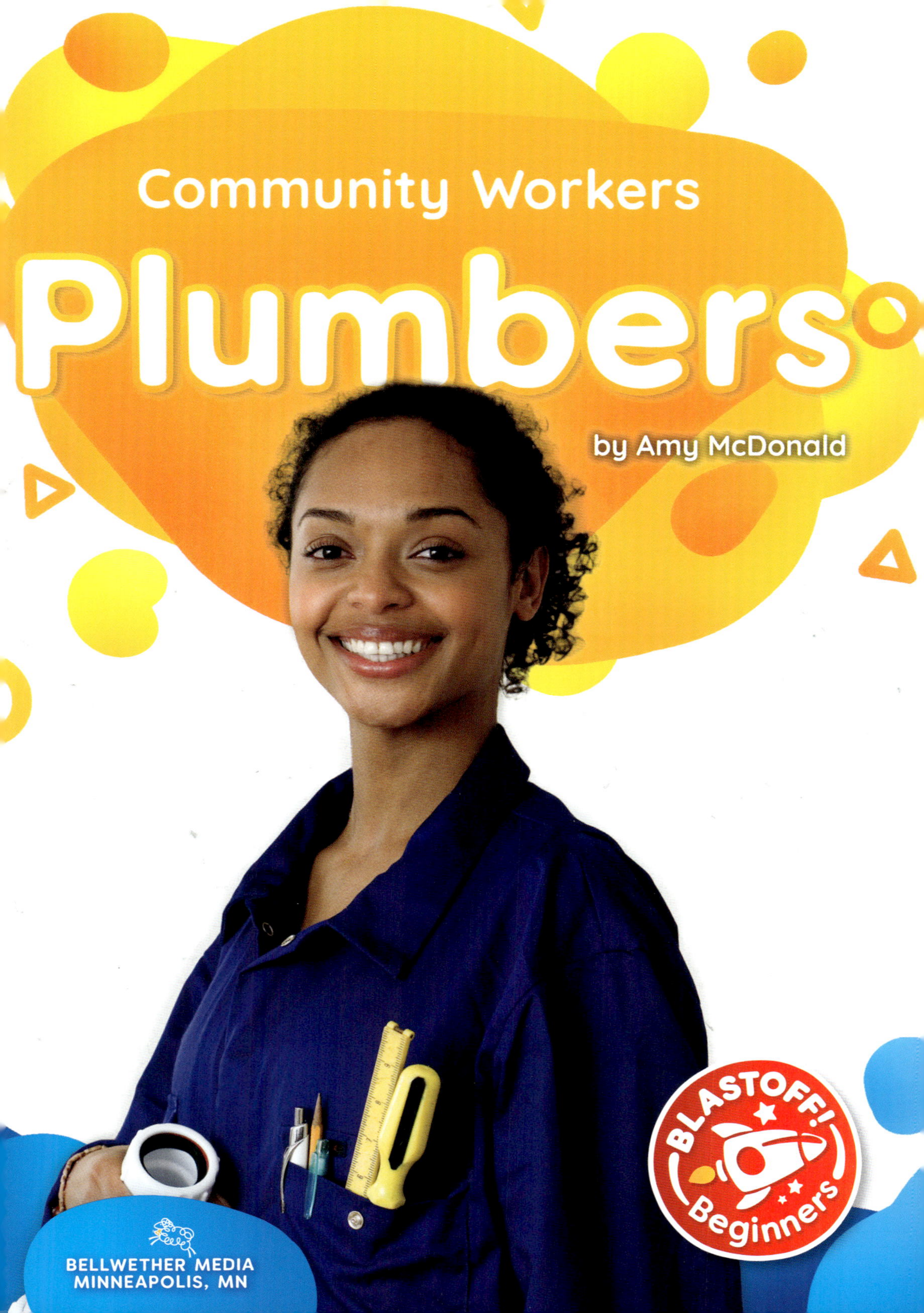
Community Workers
Plumbers
by Amy McDonald
BLASTOFF! Beginners
BELLWETHER MEDIA
MINNEAPOLIS, MN

Blastoff! Beginners are developed by literacy experts and educators to meet the needs of early readers. These engaging informational texts support young children as they begin reading about their world. Through simple language and high frequency words paired with crisp, colorful photos, Blastoff! Beginners launch young readers into the universe of independent reading.

Sight Words in This Book

and	here	them	we
big	in	they	with
get	is	to	
go	new	use	
help	the	water	

This edition first published in 2025 by Bellwether Media, Inc.

Library of Congress Cataloging-in-Publication Data

LC record for Plumbers available at: https://lccn.loc.gov/2024038074

Editor: Betsy Rathburn Designer: Laura Sowers

Printed in the United States of America, North Mankato, MN.

Table of Contents

On the Job

Drip, drip.
The plumber
is here!

What Are They?

Plumbers help water and gas flow. They work with **pipes**.

pipes

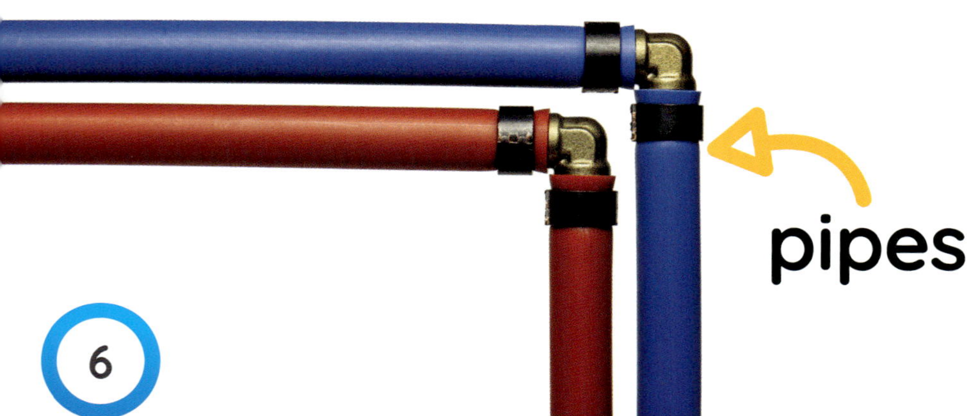

They go to houses.
They go to offices.

What Do They Do?

Plumbers put in new pipes. They fix broken pipes.

They work in small spaces. They use flashlights.

They put pipes together. They use **wrenches** and tape.

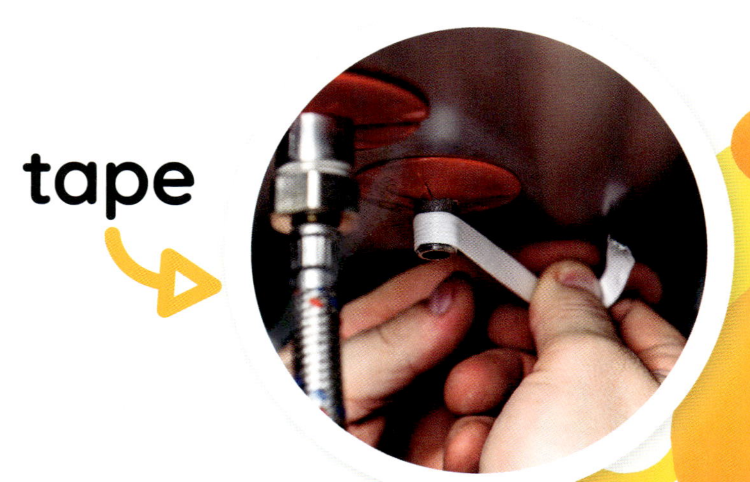

wrench

They stop **leaks**.
They use glue
or tape.

They open **clogs**. They help water get through.

Why Do We Need Them?

Plumbers fix big problems. We need them!

Plumber Facts

Tools

A Day in the Life

fix broken pipes

stop leaks

open clogs

Glossary

things that block pipes

openings where water or gas gets out

tubes used for moving water or gas

tools used to grip and turn

To Learn More

ON THE WEB

FACTSURFER

Factsurfer.com gives you a safe, fun way to find more information.

1. Go to www.factsurfer.com.
2. Enter "plumbers" into the search box and click 🔍.
3. Select your book cover to see a list of related content.

Index

The images in this book are reproduced through the courtesy of: Juice Dash, front cover; Essffes, p. 3; Andrey_Popov, pp. 4-5, 23 (leaks); John Brueske, p. 6; Monkey Business Images, pp. 6-7, 16-17, 23 (stop leaks); Stokkete, pp. 8-9; BearFotos, pp. 10-11; Muhammad Labib Adilah, p. 12; nimito, pp. 12-13; Natallia Ploskaya, p. 14; Hryshchyshen Serhii, pp. 14-15; DIGIcal, p. 16; docent, pp. 18-19; Phynart Studio, pp. 20-21; Anton Starikov, p. 22 (tape); Shamils, p. 22 (pipes); SolidMaks, p. 22 (flashlight); Dimensions, p. 23 (fix broken pipes); monkeybusinessimages, p. 23 (open clogs); ronstik, p. 23 (clogs); Oppdowngalon, p. 23 (pipes); Roman Chazov, p. 23 (wrenches).